Taylor Made

TODD TAYLOR'S MOST REQUESTED BANJO HITS

To access audio visit:
www.halleonard.com/mylibrary
Enter Code
1996-7331-7078-6872

ISBN 978-1-57424-351-2
SAN 683-8022

Cover by James Creative Group

Cover photo by Ken Marler

Copyright © 2017 CENTERSTREAM Publishing, LLC
P.O. Box 17878 - Anaheim Hills, CA 92817

www.centerstream-usa.com | centerstrm@aol.com

All rights for publication and distribution are reserved.
No part of this book may be reproduced in any form or by any Electronic or mechanical means including information storage and
retrieval systems without permission in writing from the publisher, except by reviewers who may quote brief passages in review.

Special Thanks

The Gretsch Family, Fred & Dinah Gretsch

Joe Carducci

Joe Bonsall, The Oak Ridge Boys

Mitchel Meadors
Mitchel's PlateMate
Mitchel's Tone Ring Mate
Mitchel's Archtop banjo tone rings
www.mitchelsplatemate.com

GHS Strings

Dave Cowels
Chris Walters

Joe Tyler
Mike Moody
Paul Hinton
Ken Marler
Jimmy Diresta

Photography By Ken Marler

Notation By Paul Hinton

Table of Contents

Foreword...4

Word from the Author 5

Songs:

Back Home In Carolina 6
Double C Tuning, gCGCD

Banjo Blues 12
Key of G, gDGBD

Cork Swamp Blues..15
Key of A, gDGBD, Capo 2nd Fret

Gold Tone Jubilee..18
Key of G, gDGBD

Six Guns 20
Double C Tuning, gCGCD

Taylor's Ride 24
Key of B, gDGBD, Capo 4th Fret

The Race Is On 27
Key of A, gDGBD, Capo 2nd Fret

Three-Five-N 32
Key of B, gDGBD, Capo 4th Fret

Unleashed 37
Key of G, gDGBD

Waterfall 40
Double C Tuning, gCGCD

Foreword

As a lifelong friend and personal photographer of Todd Taylor, I have had the opportunity to work with him on many projects and see firsthand the commitment and level of perfection that he demands from himself as he shares his amazing talent and flawless craft with the world. I am deeply honored to be able to share a little forward insight into this collection of Todd's greatest hits.

Since the dawn of man, music has been a driving force for humanity. It has evolved, adapted and divided into many styles and genres, each with the ability to touch the soul of a listener based on their personal taste.

Over the years, a small but ever growing group of artists have become known as "icons" or "legends" because of their innovations, pioneering and becoming influential, inspiring other artists to take chances, experiment and devote their heart and soul to their craft. Elvis Presley, Bob Marley, James Taylor, Jimi Hendrix and John Coltrane are but a few examples.

Todd Taylor has earned his place in this elite group of pioneers by blazing a trail to a style of music that is uniquely his own. It has been said that Todd Taylor is to the banjo what John Coltrane was to the saxophone. Even though Todd's roots are firmly planted in bluegrass, his heart also beats to the sound of a different drummer. Rock & roll runs through his veins and out of his fingertips, pioneering a style of music unlike any the world has ever known.

Todd's determination, extreme talent and ability to overcome obstacles has bridged the gap between bluegrass and rock & roll, a feat many said was impossible and would not work. Like the true legends that came before him, this opposition gave Todd the determination to master his craft and give the world a new genre of music that reaches across the masses. Todd became the first artist in history to take the banjo to the rock & roll top 40 on the Rick Dees show in the late '80s with his mind-blowing rendition of the classic rock hit "Free Bird".

Todd has been called "Banjovi" and the father of "newgrass". It is not certain what title history will honor Todd with, but one fact is certain: You are holding in your hand a collection of songs by a legendary artist that is pure gold and sure to become more precious, if not priceless, as time goes by. Enjoy!!

Ken Marler

Word from the Author

I am happy to share my original banjo songs with you. These are songs I have written thru the many years of my career and the most requested for tablatures.

Enjoy and have fun playing these tunes my friends.

Happy Picking.

Todd Taylor

5 Time Grammy Nominee
Guinness World Record's Fastest Banjo Player

Back Home In Carolina

Double C tuning

Composed by Todd Taylor

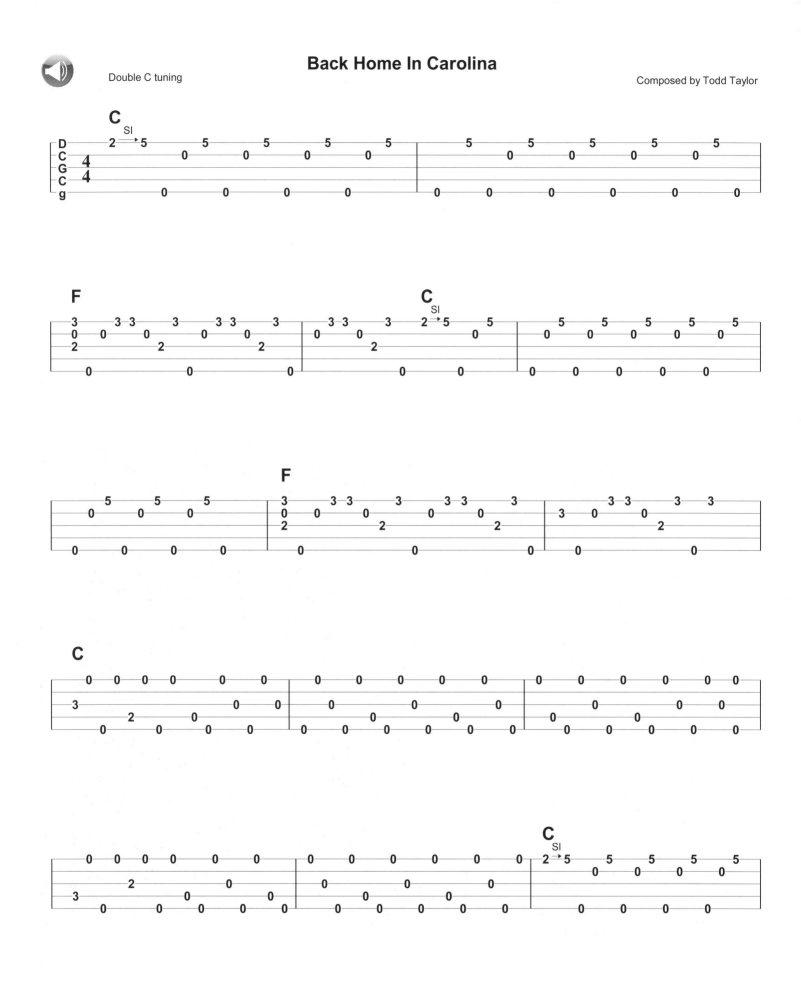

Copyright by Todd Taylor, Used by Permission.

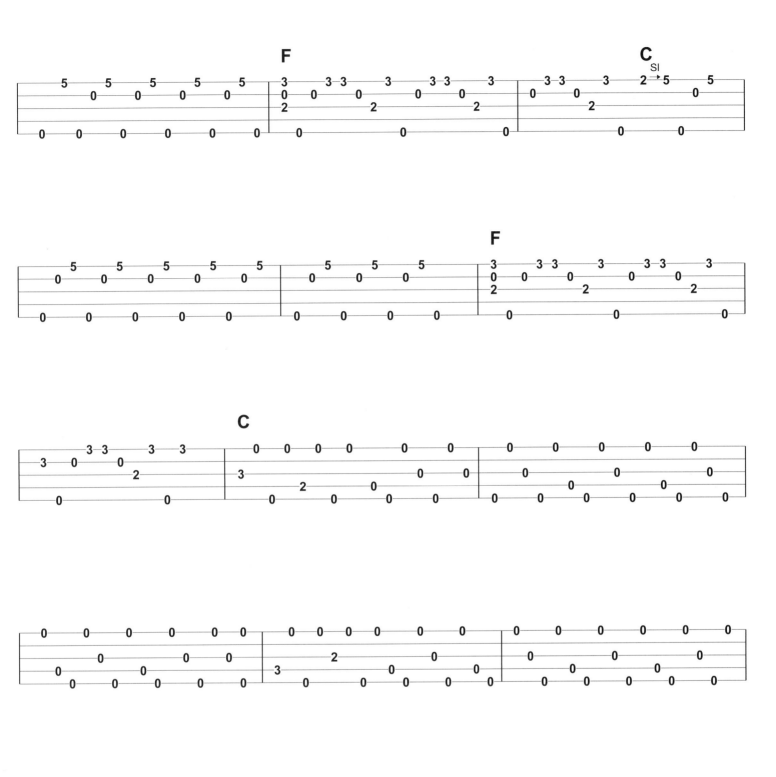

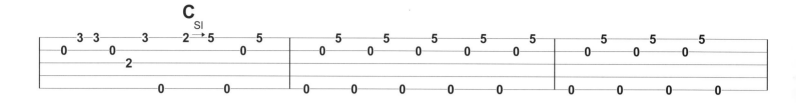

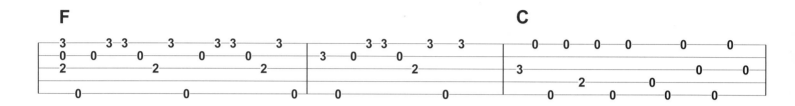

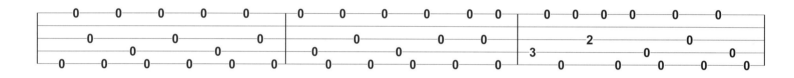

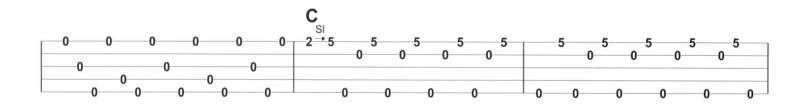

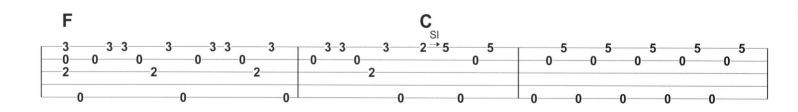

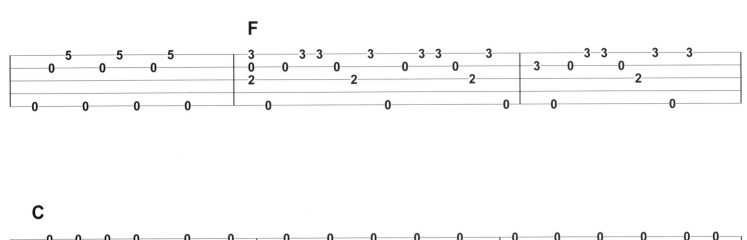

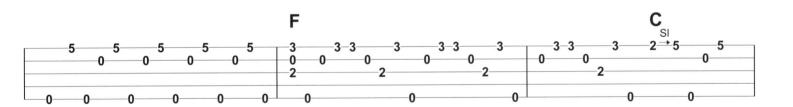

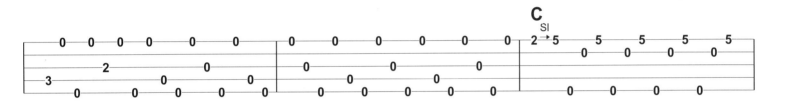

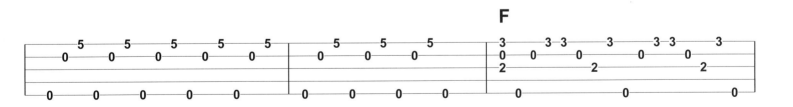

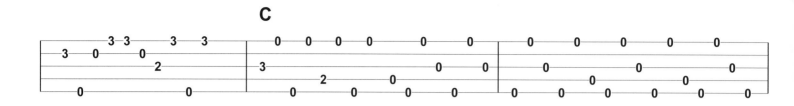

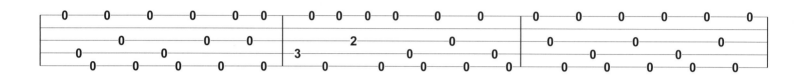

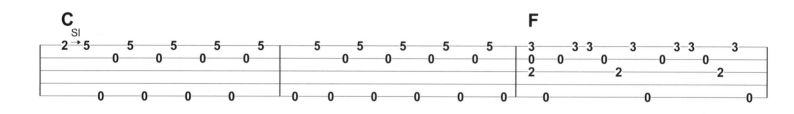

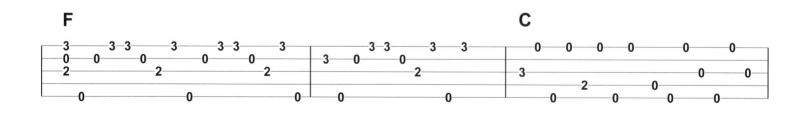

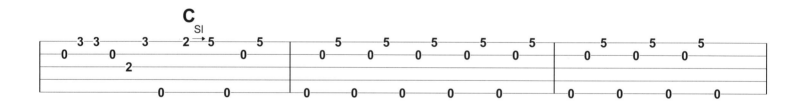

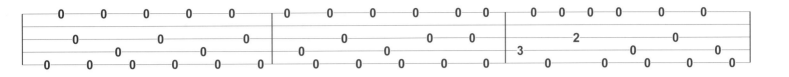

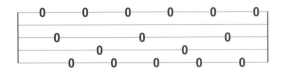

Todd Taylor and Jimmy Diresta at Streetsound, Brooklyn, NY.

Banjo Blues

Key of G

Composed by Todd Taylor

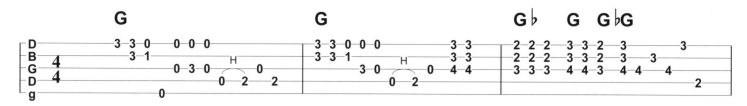

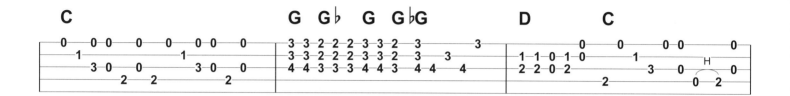

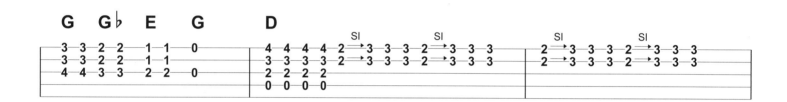

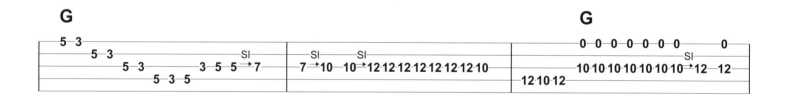

Copyright by Todd Taylor, Used by Permission.

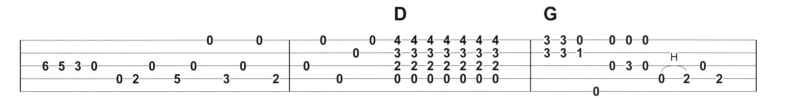

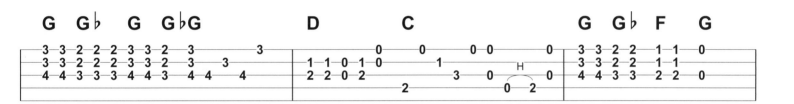

G

```
|--1715--------------------------------|----------------------|---------------0-------0----|
|----1715------------------------------|----------------------|----------------------------|
|------1715------15171517171515--------|12121010106 5 3 6 5 3 0 6 5 3 0|6 5 3 0----0----0----0-|
|----------171517----------------------|----------------------|--------0 2----5----3----2--|
```

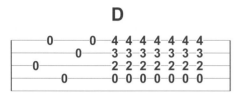

D

```
|----0------0--4 4 4 4 4 4 4-|
|-------0------3 3 3 3 3 3 3-|
|--0-----------2 2 2 2 2 2 2-|
|-------0------0 0 0 0 0 0 0-|
```

Cork Swamp Blues

Key of A (capo 2nd fret)

Composed by Todd Taylor

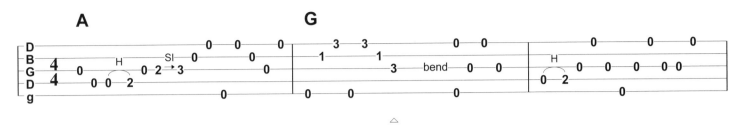

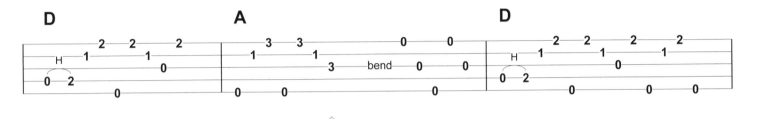

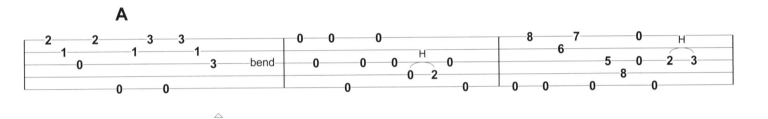

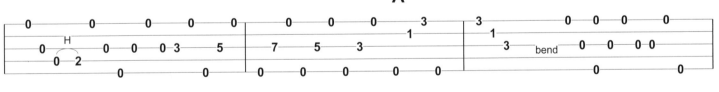

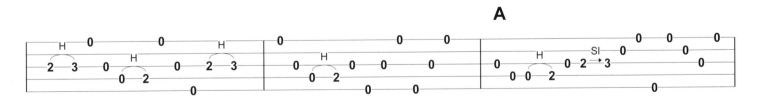

Copyright by Todd Taylor, Used by Permission.

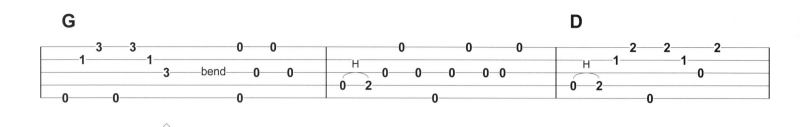

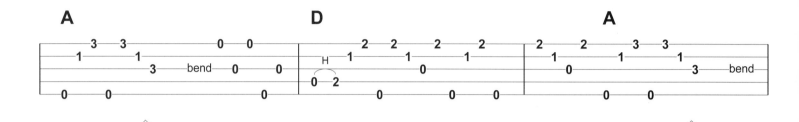

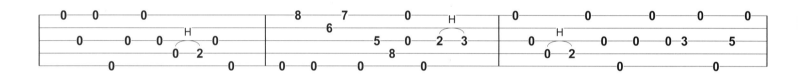

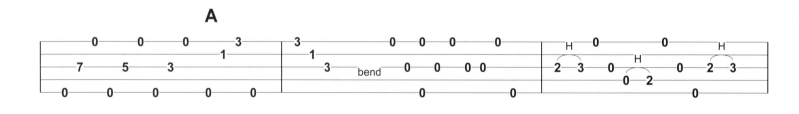

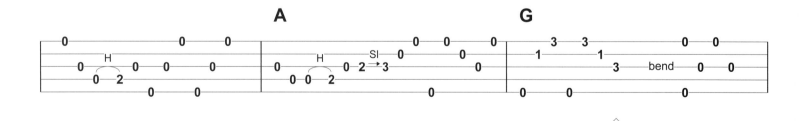

16

G

```
-1715-------------------------------------------------------------------|----------------------------0-------0--------
----1715-----------------------------------------------------------------|-------------------------------------------
------1715--------15171517171515--|--1212101010 6 5 3 6 5 3 0 6 5 3 0--|--6 5 3 0----------0----0------0------------
--------171517-----------------------|------------------------------------------|-------------0 2-------5-----3-----2--
```

D

```
----0--------0--4-4-4-4-4-4-4----
-------0--------3-3-3-3-3-3-3----
--0-------------2-2-2-2-2-2-2----
-------0--------0-0-0-0-0-0-0----
```

Todd Taylor playing live on Justin Reed Show.

Gold Tone Jubilee

Key of G

Composed by Todd Taylor

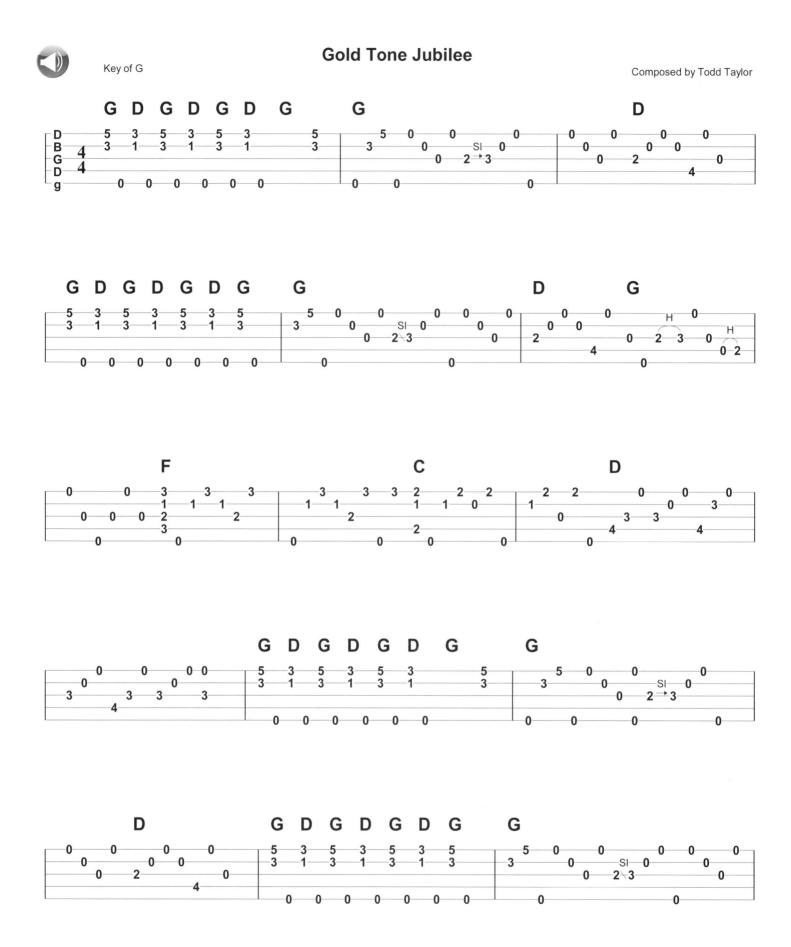

Copyright by Todd Taylor, Used by Permission.

18

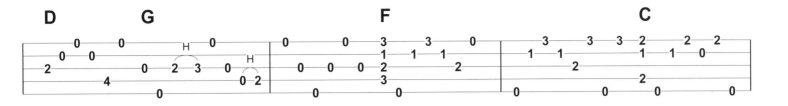

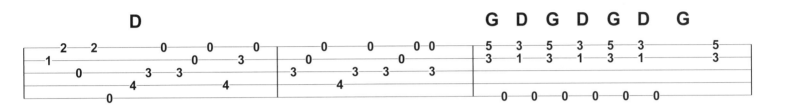

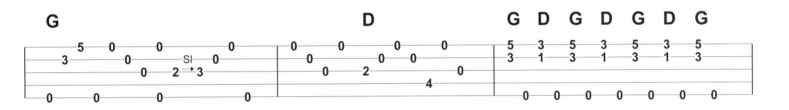

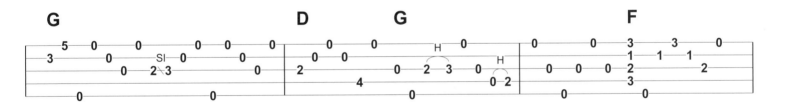

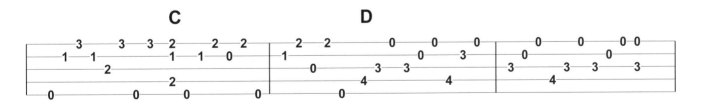

Six Guns

Double C tuning

Copmpsed by Todd Taylor

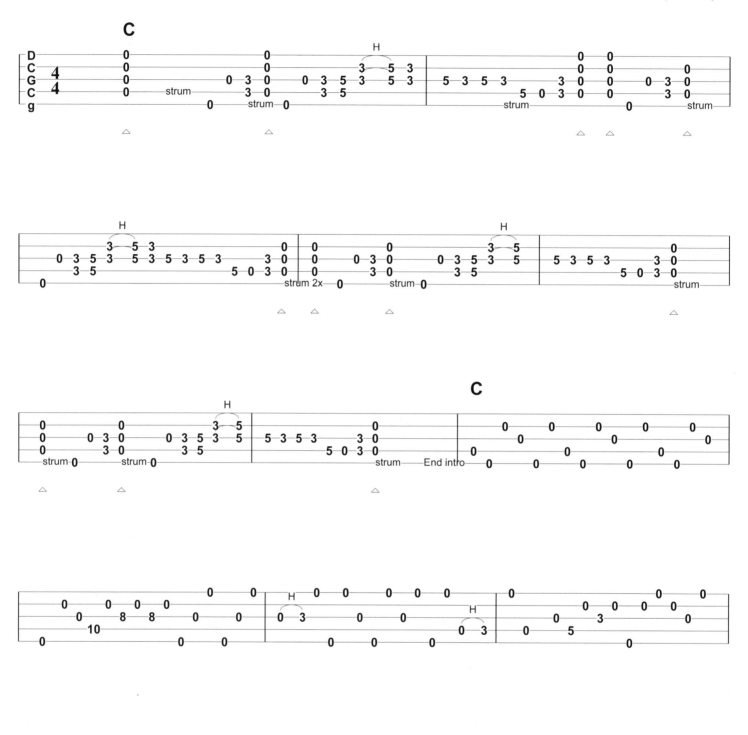

Copyright by Todd Taylor, Used by Permission.

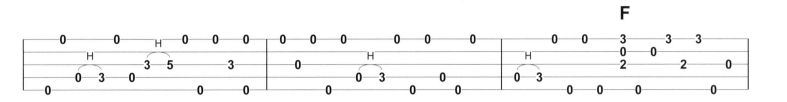

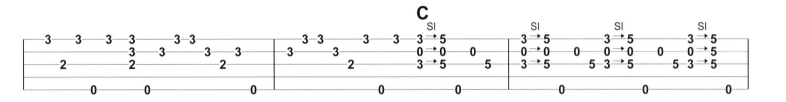

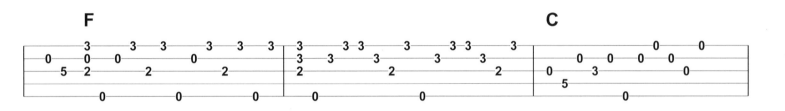

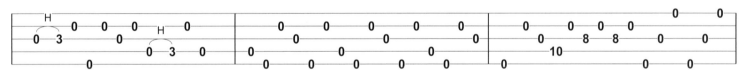

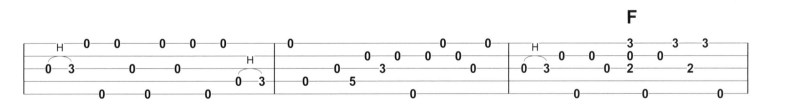

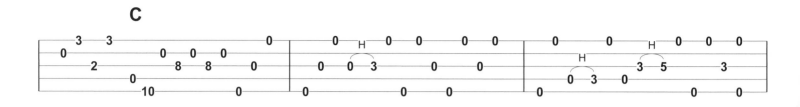

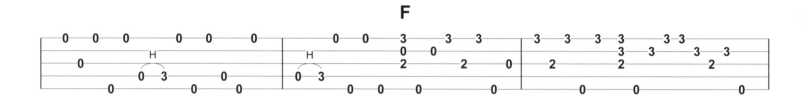

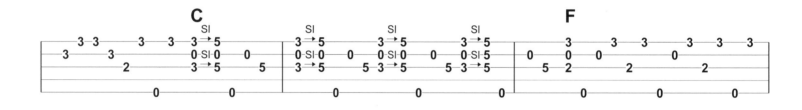

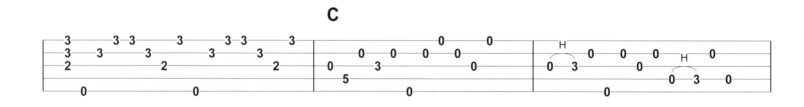

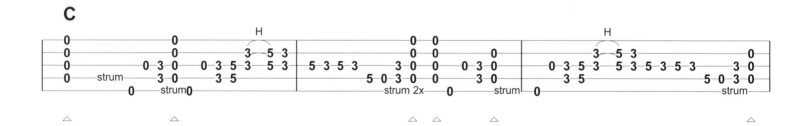

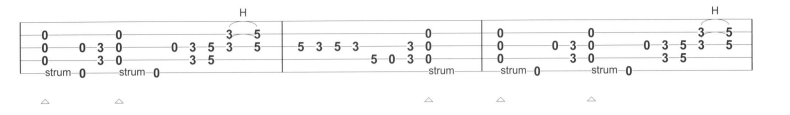

Todd with Joe Carducci & Tom Petersson of Cheap Trick.

Taylor's Ride

Key of B (capo 4th fret)

Composed by Todd Taylor

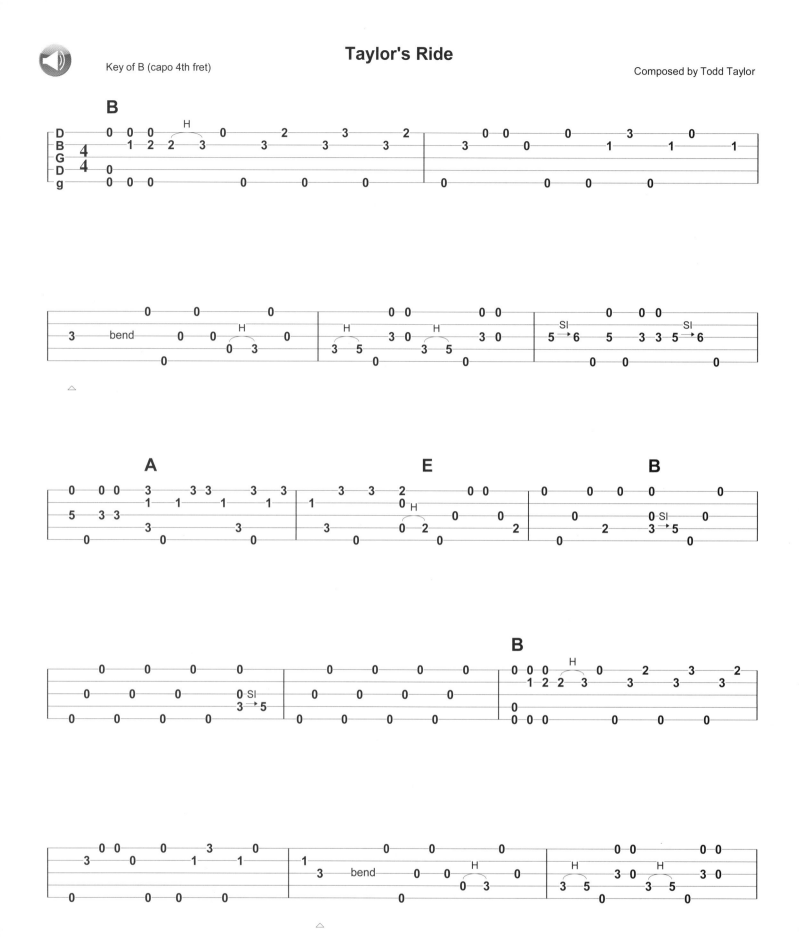

Copyright by Todd Taylor, Used by Permission.

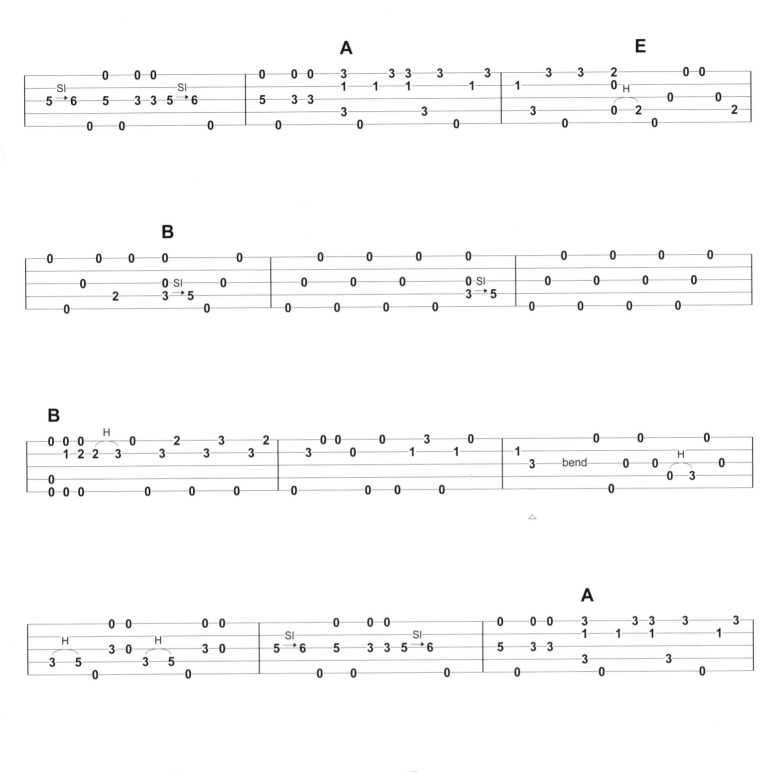

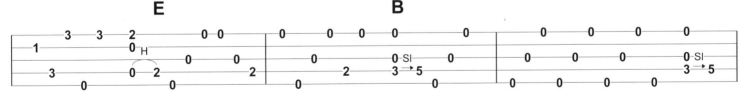

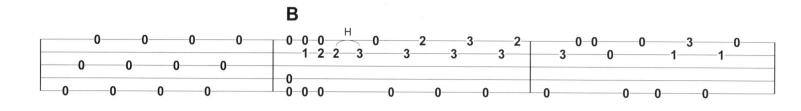

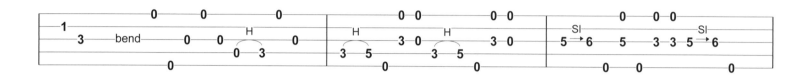

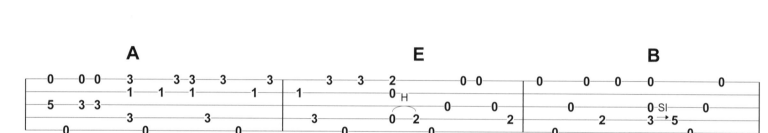

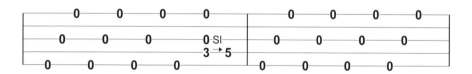

The Race Is On

Key of A (capo 2nd fret)

Composed by Todd Taylor

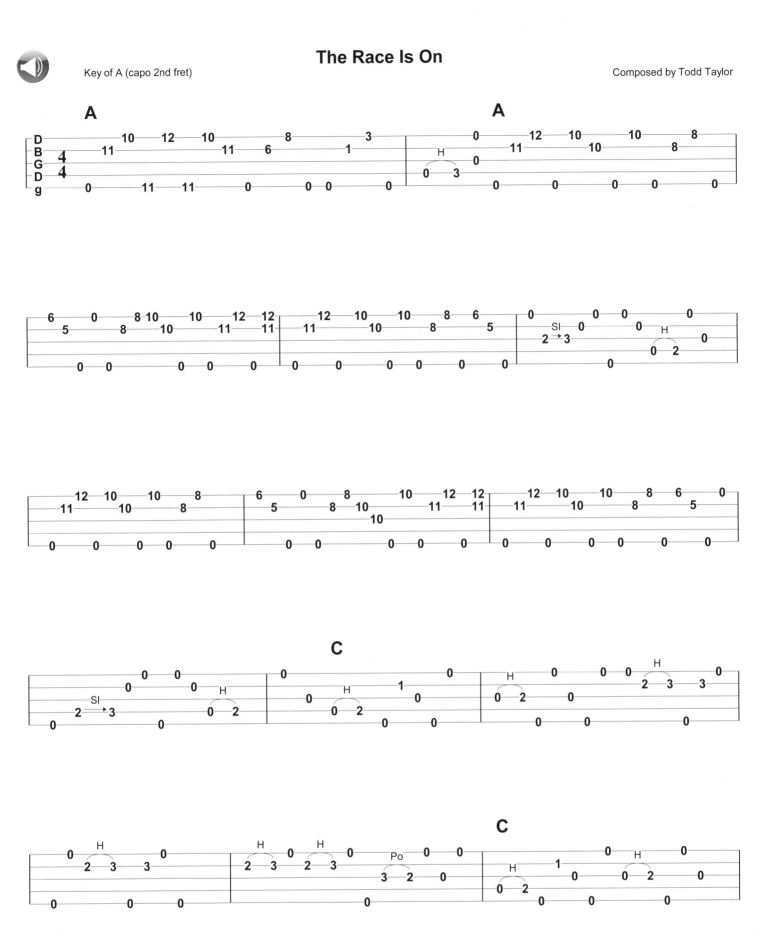

Copyright by Todd Taylor, Used by Permission.

27

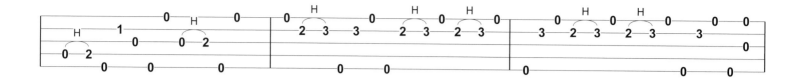

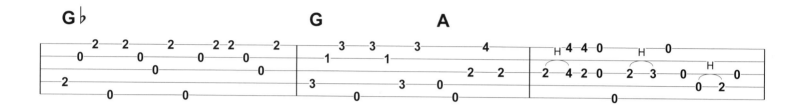

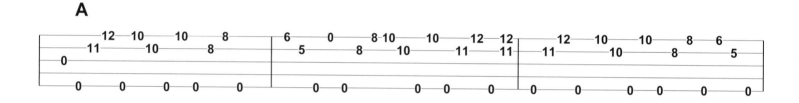

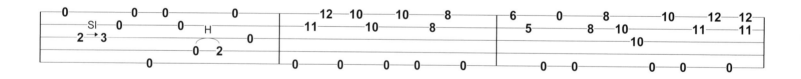

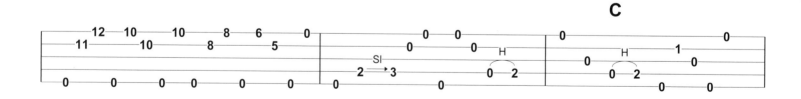

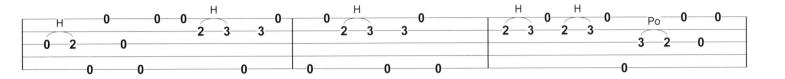

C

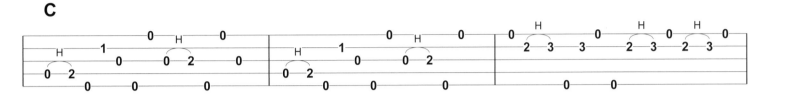

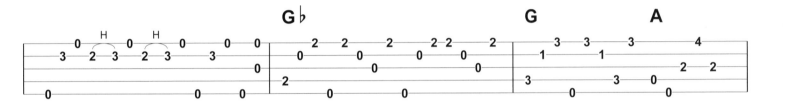

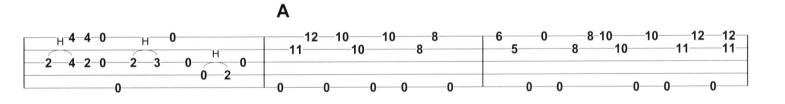

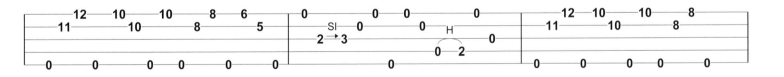

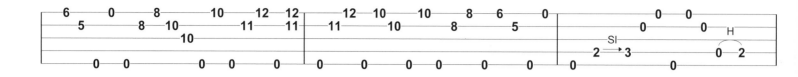

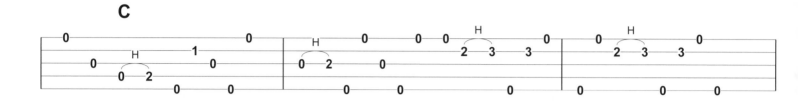

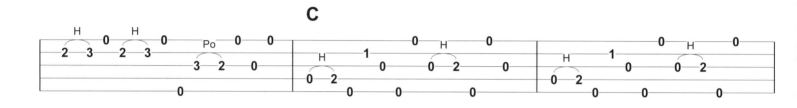

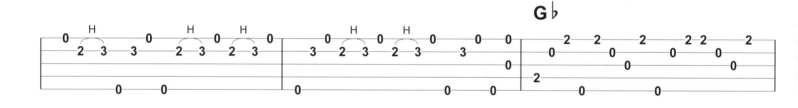

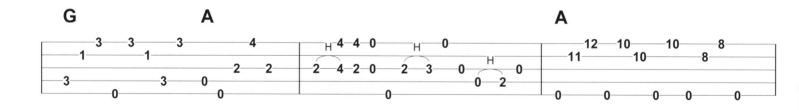

30

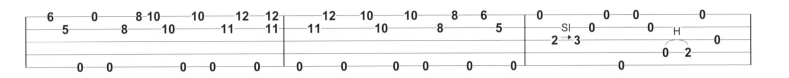

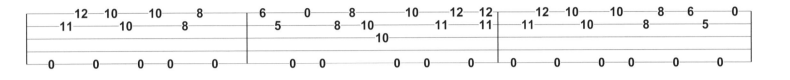

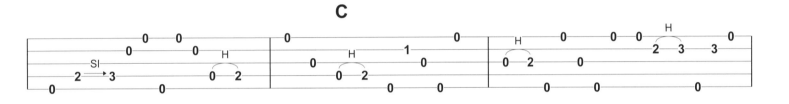

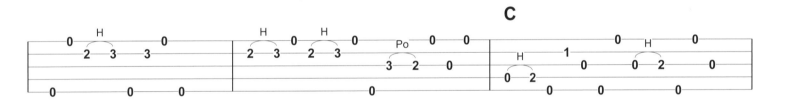

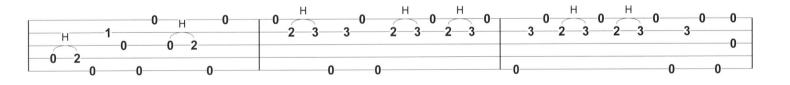

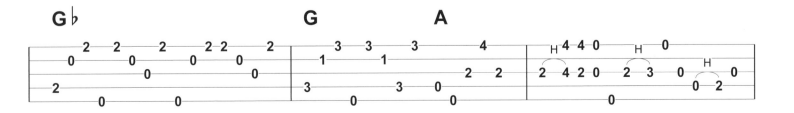

31

Three-Five-N

Key of B (capo 4th fret)

Composed by Todd Taylor

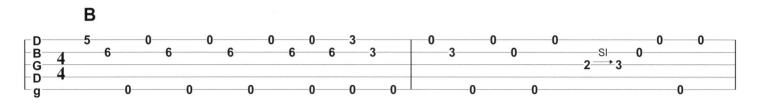

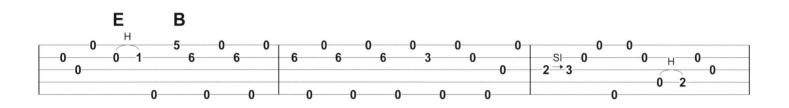

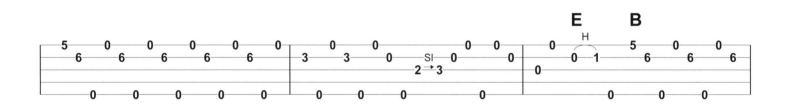

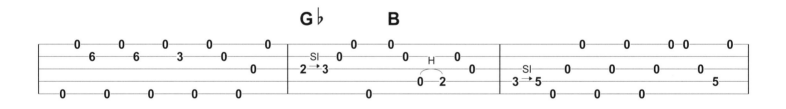

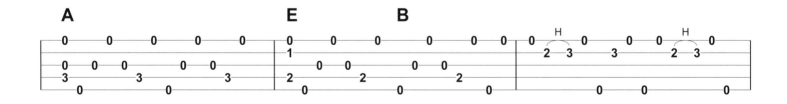

Copyright by Todd Taylor, Used by Permission.

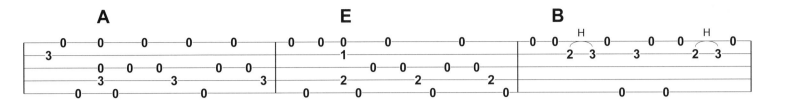

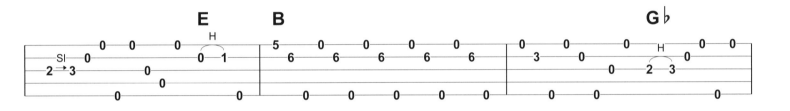

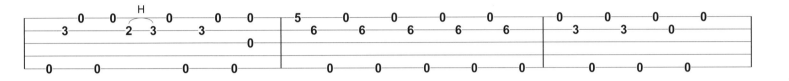

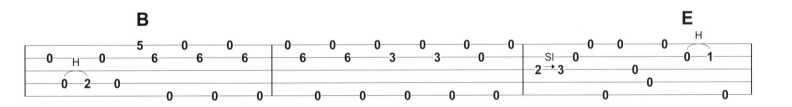

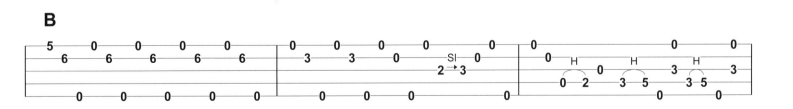

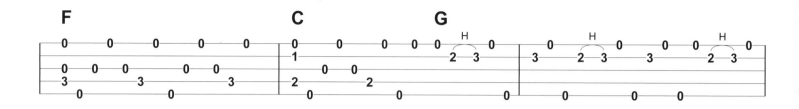

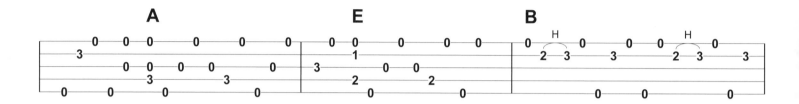

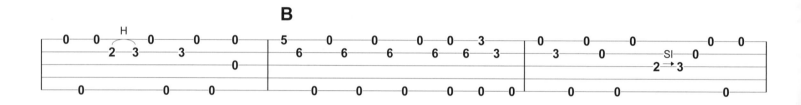

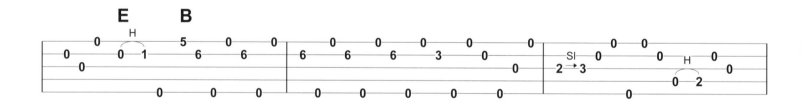

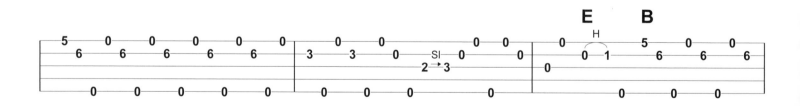

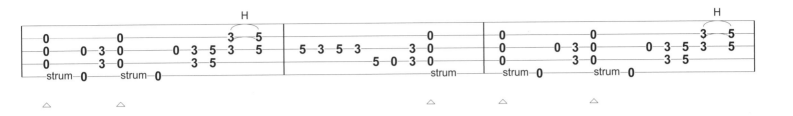

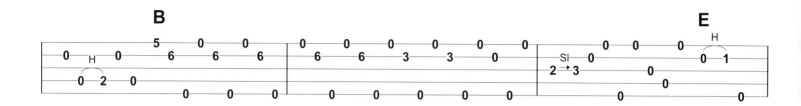

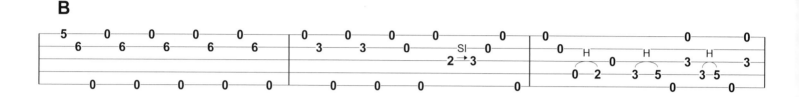

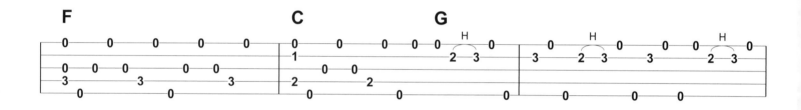

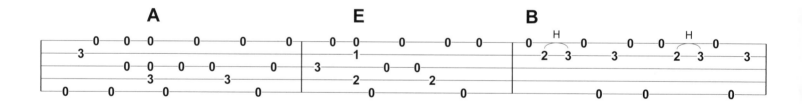

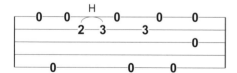

Unleashed

Key of G

Composed by Todd Taylor

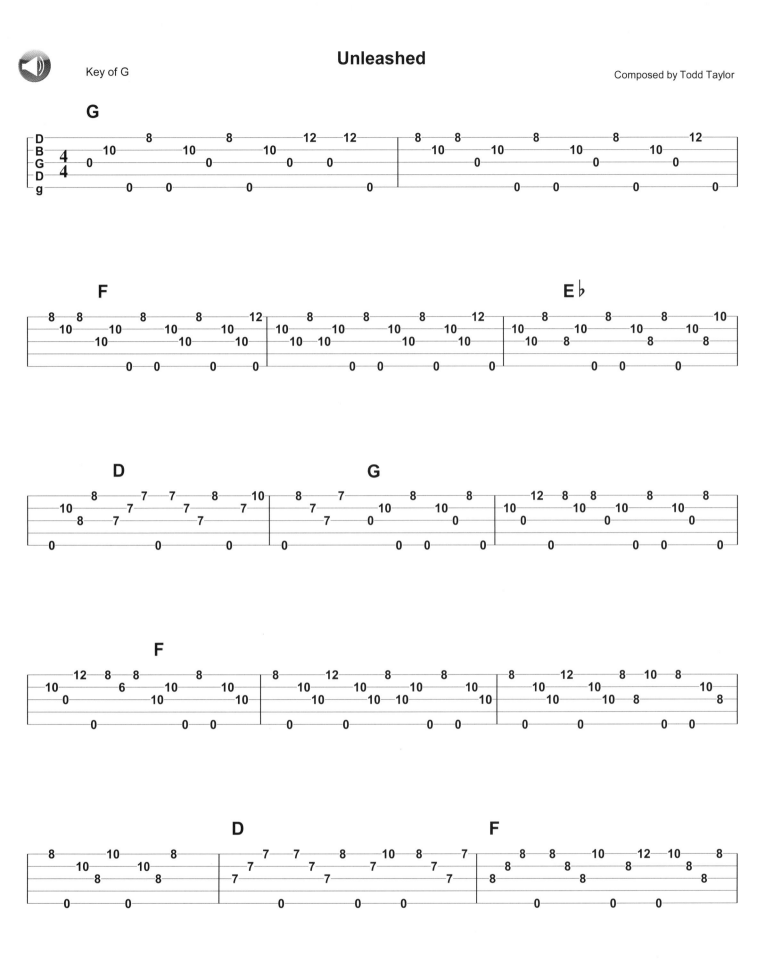

Copyright by Todd Taylor, Used by Permission.

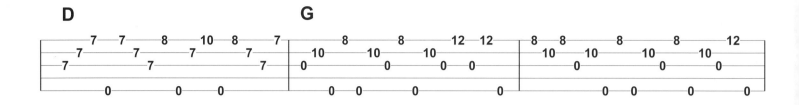

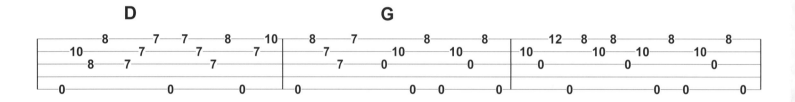

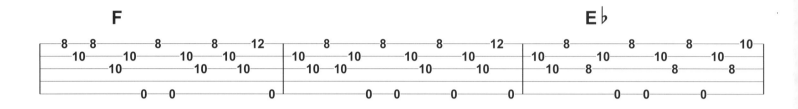

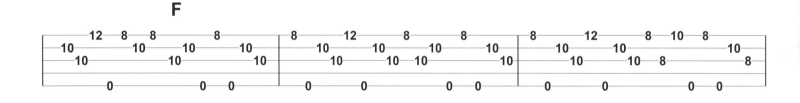

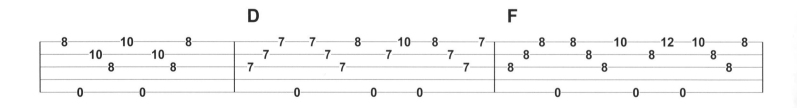

D **G**

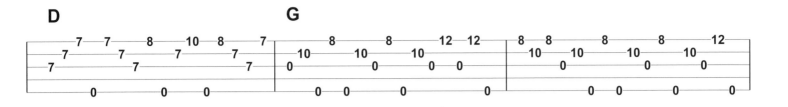

F **E♭**

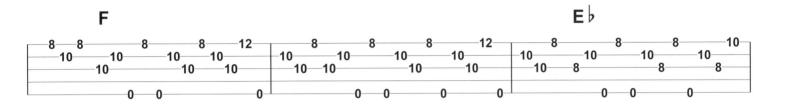

D **G**

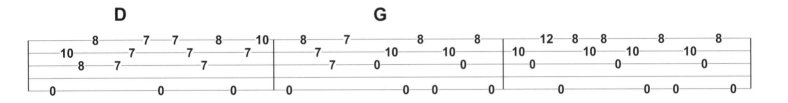

F

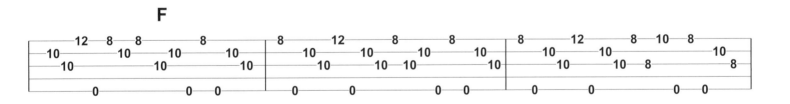

D **F**

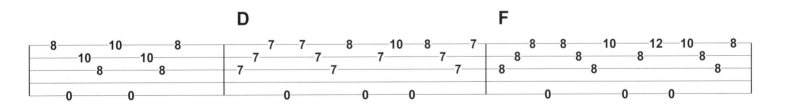

D

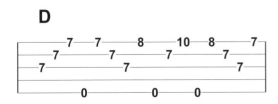

Waterfall

Double C tuning

Composed by Todd Taylor

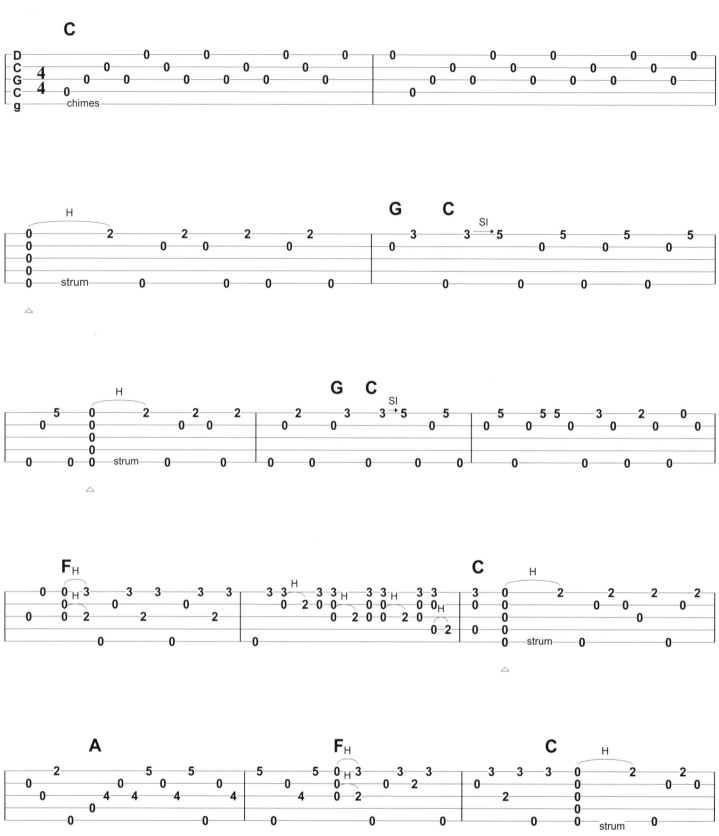

Copyright by Todd Taylor, Used by Permission.

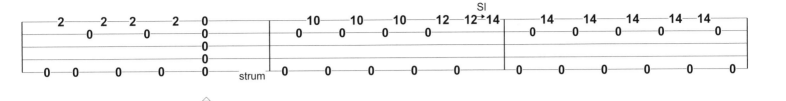

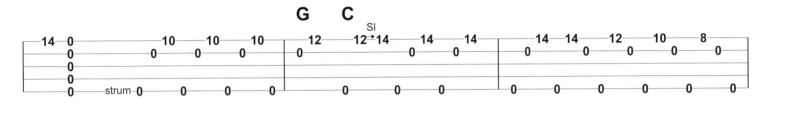

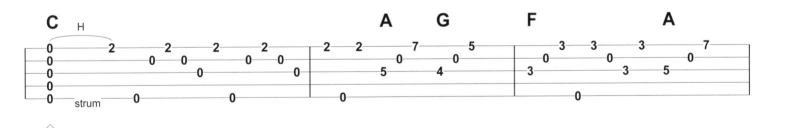

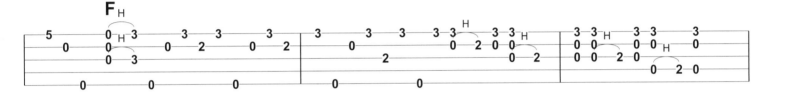

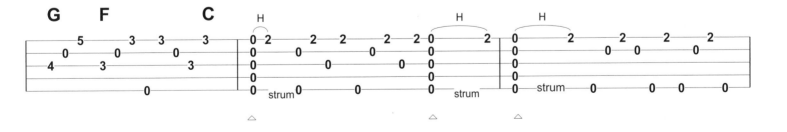

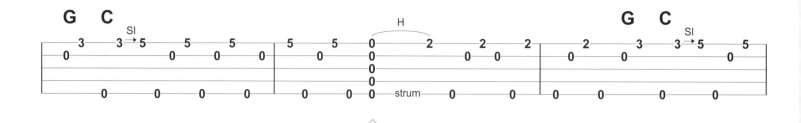

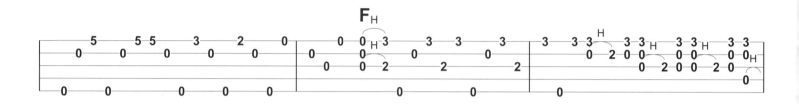

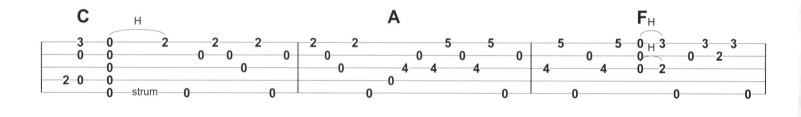

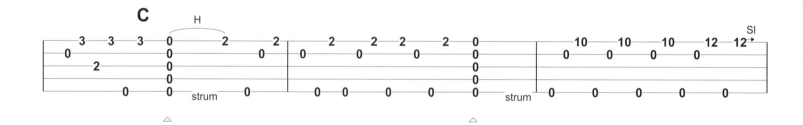

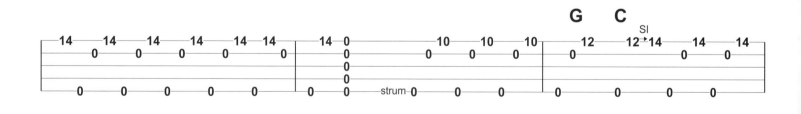

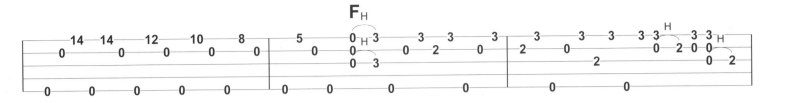

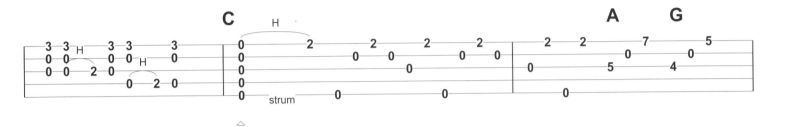

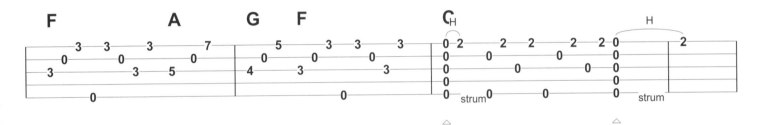

Todd on stage.

Todd and Joe Bonsall of the Oak Ridge Boys.

Todd Taylor and Fred Gretsch.

Thornton Cline and Todd in Todd's recording studio.

More Great Banjo Books from Todd Taylor...

PICKIN' OVER THE SPEED LIMIT
Guinness World Records Fastest Banjo Player
Presented by Todd Taylor
Centerstream Publishing is proud to present Todd Taylor's incredible arrangements in notes & banjo tab of classics including: Dust in the Wind; El Cumbachero; Freebird; How Great Thou Art; I Can't Stop Loving You; Norwegian Wood; Rocket Man; Wayfaring Stranger, Yakety Sax; and more, plus some of Todd's terrific originals. The book includes a bonus CD of Todd's masterful playing on six searing tracks. An absolute must for all banjo players.
00001494 .... $19.99

TODD TAYLOR'S BANJO CHRISTMAS
by Todd Taylor
Exciting arrangements by banjo virtuoso Todd Taylor that are both challenging and fun to play; sure to become your favorites. The music is in standard G Tuning. Listen to the CD to hear how the banjo should sound and play along with the note-for-note tablature of each song. A perennial feast of banjo music to enjoy now and to rediscover year after year. So lets tune up, spread the cheer and play. Intermediate to Advance level.
00149966 .... $19.99

TODD TAYLOR'S GOSPEL BANJO
Foreword by Fred Gretsch
by Todd Taylor
This book features ten exciting arrangements of favorite gospel classics by virtuoso Todd "Banjoman" Taylor. Just follow the easy tab, listen to the audio and play along with Todd quickly and easily! Songs include: Amazing Grace • How Great Thou Art • Uncloudy Day • What a Friend We Have in Jesus • When the Roll is Called Up Yonder • I'll Fly Away and more.
00196586 .... $19.99

P.O. Box 17878 - Anaheim Hills, CA 92817
(714) 779-9390   www.centerstream-usa.com

More Great Banjo Books from Centerstream...

BEGINNING CLAWHAMMER BANJO
DVD
by Ken Perlman

Ken Perlman is one of the most celebrated clawhammer banjo stylists performing today. In this new DVD, he teaches how to play this exciting style, with ample close-ups and clear explanations of techniques such as: hand positions, chords, tunings, brush-thumb, single-string strokes, hammer-ons, pull-offs and slides. Songs include: Boatsman • Cripple Creek • Pretty Polly. Includes a transcription booklet. 60 minutes.

00000330 DVD $19.95

INTERMEDIATE CLAWHAMMER BANJO
DVD
by Ken Perlman

Picking up where *Beginning Clawhammer Banjo* leaves off, this DVD begins with a review of brush thumbing and the single-string stroke, then moves into specialized techniques such as: drop- and double-thumbing, single-string brush thumb, chords in double "C" tuning, and more. Tunes include: Country Waltz • Green Willis • Little Billie Wilson • Magpie • The Meeting of the Waters • Old Joe Clark • and more! Includes a transcription booklet. 60 minutes.

00000331 DVD $19.95

CLAWHAMMER STYLE BANJO
INCLUDES TAB DVD
A Complete Guide for Beginning and Advanced Banjo Players
by Ken Perlman

This handbook covers basic right & left-hand positions, simple chords, and fundamental clawhammer techniques: the brush, the "bumm-titty" strum, pull-offs, and slides. There is also instruction on more complicated picking, double thumbing, quick slides, fretted pull-offs, harmonics, improvisation, and more. Includes over 40 fun-to-play banjo tunes.

00000118 Book Only..$19.95
00000334 DVD $39.95

THE EARLY MINSTREL BANJO
INCLUDES TAB
by Joe Weidlich

Featuring more than 65 classic songs, this interesting book teaches how to play the minstrel banjo like players who were part of various popular troupes in 1865. The book includes: a short history of the banjo, including the origins of the minstrel show; info on the construction of minstrel banjos, chapters on each of the seven major banjo methods published through the end of the Civil War; songs from each method in banjo tablature, many available for the first time; info on how to arrange songs for the minstrel banjo; a reference list of contemporary gut and nylon string gauges approximating historical banjo string tensions in common usage during the antebellum period (for those Civil War re-enactors who wish to achieve that old-time "minstrel banjo" sound); an extensive cross-reference list of minstrel banjo song titles found in the major antebellum banjo methods; and more. (266 pages)

00000325..$29.95

MELODIC CLAWHAMMER BANJO
A Comprehensive Guide to Modern Clawhammer Banjo
by Ken Perlman

Ken Perlman, today's foremost player of the style, brings you this comprehensive guide to the melodic clawhammer. Over 50 tunes in clear tablature. Learn to play authentic versions of Appalachian fiddle tunes, string band tunes, New England hornpipes, Irish jigs, Scottish reels, and more. Includes arrangements by many important contemporary players, and chapters on basic and advanced techniques. Also features over 70 musical illustrations, plus historical notes, and period photos.

00000412 Book/CD Pack $19.95

MINSTREL BANJO – BRIGGS' BANJO INSTRUCTOR
INCLUDES TAB
by Joseph Weidlich

The Banjo Instructor by Tom Briggs, published in 1855, was the first complete method for banjo. It contained "many choice plantation melodies," "a rare collection of quaint old dances," and the "elementary principles of music." This edition is a reprinting of the original Briggs' *Banjo Instructor*, made up-to-date with modern explanations, tablature, and performance notes. It teaches how to hold the banjo, movements, chords, slurs and more, and includes 68 banjo solo songs that Briggs presumably learned directly from slaves.

00000221..$12.95

MORE MINSTREL BANJO
INCLUDES TAB
by Joseph Weidlich

This is the second book in a 3-part series of intabulations of music for the minstrel (Civil War-era) banjo. Adapted from Frank Converse's *Banjo Instructor, Without a Master* (published in New York in 1865), this book contains a choice collection of banjo solos, jigs, songs, reels, walk arounds, and more, progressively arranged and plainly explained, enabling players to become proficient banjoists. Thorough measure-by-measure explanations are provided for each of the songs, all of which are part of the traditional minstrel repertoire.

00000258..$12.95

WITH MY BANJO ON MY KNEE
The Minstrel Songs of Stephen Foster
arr. for banjo by Daniel Partner
Historical notes by Edwin J. Sims

Here are some of the first and most popular songs ever written for banjo. Fascinating historical notes accompany this collection, describing the meaning of the songs, their place in history, the significance of the musicians who first performed them, and Foster himself, America's first professional songwriter. The complete original lyrics of each song and an extensive bibliography are included. The CD contains recordings of each arrangement performed on solo minstrel banjo.

00001179 Book/CD Pack $19.95

CENTERSTREAM®

P.O. Box 17878 - Anaheim Hills, CA 92817
(714) 779-9390   www.centerstream-usa.com

More Great Banjo Books from Centerstream...

400 SMOKIN' BLUEGRASS BANJO LICKS

by Eddie Collins

Know only 20 solo licks? How about 50? 100? 200? If that's all, then you need this book, designed to help you improvise bluegrass style solos. 400 licks are played over standard chord progressions; the use of licks sometimes will take precedent over stating the melody. The progressions used are based primarily on common vocal numbers. Some of the licks included are: chromatic licks, embellishing a fiddletune, high position licks, Reno style, pentatonic blues, boogie licks, swing phrasing, sequential licks, back-up licks and many more. Uses standard G tuning. Companion book: 400 Smokin Bluegrass Guitar Licks (#00123172).
00123175 Book/CD Pack...$19.99

GIBSON MASTERTONE
Flathead 5-String Banjos of the 1930's and 1940's
by Jim Mills

While Gibson produced literally thousands of banjos prior to WWII, only 250 or so featured that "Magic Combination" of an Original Flathead Tonering and Five-string neck. 19 of the absolute best are featured here. With details of their known histories and provenances, as well as never-before-seen photos, bills of sale, factory shipping ledgers, and other ephemera relating to these rare and highly desirable instruments..
00001241 Full Color Softcover $45.00

FORTY GOSPEL GREATS FOR BANJO
by Eddie Collins

When you hear the term "Gospel Banjo," many assume we are talking about tunes you hear at every bluegrass festival-tunes in the Southern Gospel tradition. While these definitely make for good banjo fare, Eddie sought to cover new ground, of the 40 popular songs included, nearly 20 of them have not been previously arranged for banjo, plus lyrics have been placed below each melody note to give the player a sense of when to stress notes in order to bring out the melody above the fill-notes of the rolls. Each song is played on the enclosed CD. These 40 Gospel Greats for Banjo are both enjoyable and inspirational.
00001497 Book/CD Pack...$19.99

CELTIC SONGS FOR THE TENOR BANJO
37 Traditional Songs and Instrumentals
by Dick Sheridan

Jigs & reels, hornpipes, airs, dances and more are showcased in this exciting 37 collection drawn from Ireland, Scotland, Wales, Cornwall, Brittany and the Isle of Man. Each traditional song – with its lilting melody and rich accompaniment harmony – has been carefully selected and presented for tenor banjo in both note form and tablature with chord symbols and diagrams. Lyrics and extra verses are included for many songs. Includes: All Through The Night, Blackbird Will You Go, The Campbells Are Coming, Garry Owen, Harvest Home, O'Gallaher's Frolics, Saddle The Pony, Swallow Tail Jig and many more.
00122477...$14.99

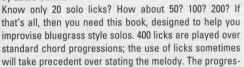

OLD TIME STRING BAND BANJO STYLES
by Joseph Weidlich

POld Time String Band Banjo Styles will introduce you to the traditional, rural string band banjo styles as played in the southern mountains of the eastern United States, which were used to "second" vocal songs and fiddle tunes during the Golden Age of recorded string band music, from the early 1920s through the early 1930s. Includes: Historical Background , String Band Transcriptions of Selected Backups and Solos, Building a Thumb-lead Style Backup.
00123693...$19.99

TRAD JAZZ FOR TENOR BANJO

by Dick Sheridan

Part of a universal repertoire familiar to all traditional jazz musicians, the 35 standards in this collection are arranged for the tenor banjo but chord symbols make playing suitable for all banjo tunings as well as other chord instruments. Popular keys have been chosen, with melodies in notes and tab, plus large, easy-to-read chord diagrams, lyrics, commentary and more. Includes: Margie, Wabash Blues, Tishmigo Blues, Avalon, Shine, Back Home Again in Indiana, Shinny like My Sister Kate, St. Louis Blues, Jazz Me Blues, Old Green River, By and By, Yellow Dog Blues and more.
00139419 Book/CD Pack...$19.99

BOB CARLIN - FIDDLE TUNES FOR CLAWHAMMER BANJO
by Bob Carlin

Renowned instructor and Grammy nominee Bob Carlin is one of the best-known banjoists performing today. This book, an update of his 1983 classic with the welcome addition of a CD, teaches readers how to play 32 best-loved pieces from his first two solo recordings: Fiddle Tunes for Clawhammer Banjo and Where Did You Get That Hat? Includes fantastic photos from throughout Bob's career.
00001327 Book/CD Pack...$19.99

GOSPEL BANJO
arranged by Dennis Caplinger

Features 15 spiritual favorites, each arranged in 2 different keys for banjo. Includes: Amazing Grace, Crying Holy, I'll Fly Away, In the Sweet By and By, Just a Closer Walk with Thee, Life's Railway to Heaven, Nearer My God to Thee, Old Time Religion, Swing Low, Sweet Chariot, Wayfaring Stranger, Will the Circle Be Unbroken, more!
00000249...$12.95

5 STRING BANJO NATURAL STYLE
No Preservatives
by Ron Middlebrook

Now available with a helpful play-along CD, this great songbook for 5-string banjo pickers features 10 easy, 10 intermediate and 10 difficult arrangements of the most popular bluegrass banjo songs. This book/CD pack comes complete with a chord chart.
00000284...$17.95

P.O. Box 17878 - Anaheim Hills, CA 92817

(714) 779-9390   www.centerstream-usa.com

Those using
Centerstream
Books & DVDs

The Competition